December, 2008

Ted,

It took a "flat lander" from Connecticut to make Vermont Vermont!

Love
Dad

THE QUOTABLE
Ethan Allen

STATUE OF ETHAN ALLEN BY VERMONT ARTIST LARKIN MEAD, AT THE STATE HOUSE, 1861.

THE QUOTABLE

Ethan Allen

EDITED BY

J. Kevin Graffagnino

H. Nicholas Muller III

Vermont Historical Society

Library of Congress Cataloging-in-Publication Data

The quotable Ethan Allen / edited by J. Kevin Graffagnino, H. Nicholas Muller III.

p. cm.

Includes bibliographical references.

ISBN 0-934720-52-5 (alk. paper)

1. Allen, Ethan, 1738-1789--Quotations. 2. Soldiers--United States--Quotations. 3. Pioneers--Vermont--Quotations. 4. Vermont--History--Revolution, 1775-1783--Quotations, maxims, etc. 5. United States--History--Revolution, 1775-1783--Quotations, maxims, etc. I. Allen, Ethan, 1738-1789. II. Graffagnino, J. Kevin. III. Muller, H. N. IV. Vermont Historical Society.

E207.A4A25 2005

974.3′03′092--dc22

2005012955

Printed in the United States of America

07 06 05 1 2 3

First printing, June 2005

ISBN: 0-934720-52-5

Printer: Capital City Press

Cover and Text Design, Composition: Carrie Fradkin/C Design

Typeface: Centaur

Printed on Glatfelter paper

In Appreciation

of

Lois H. McClure

Our Friend

and

Generous Supporter

of the

Vermont Historical Society

and the

Ethan Allen Homestead

Contents

Introduction

Over two centuries after his death in February 1789, Ethan Allen remains the most widely acclaimed and best-known Vermonter. Revered for his bold actions, commanding physical prowess, and unwavering assertion of Vermont independence, he earned his status as a genuine folk hero during his lifetime. Without his dynamic presence on the New Hampshire Grants in the 1770s, New York might extend east to the Connecticut River; separatists in the Wyoming region of northeastern Pennsylvania called on him to lead them in the mid-1780s; and near the end of his life the Shaysite rebels in Massachusetts tried to enlist him to head their motley army. "There is an original something about him," George Washington said of Ethan, and many others in Ethan's own generation agreed. Probably the only Vermonter widely recognized outside the Green Mountain State, Allen is Vermont's counterpart to Daniel Boone, Davy Crockett, Kit Carson, and Wyatt Earp in the annals of American frontier history.

In Vermont, Ethan Allen and the Green Mountain Boys he organized and led have become enduring icons. The subject of multiple novels, children's books, and biographies, Allen has loaned his cachet to a bowling alley, a motel, gas stations, a fire company, an exclusive private club, a medical center, a launderette, a distinguished national chain of furniture stores, an optical company, and more. The Vermont Air National Guard proudly calls itself the Green Mountain Boys, representing, they believe, the independent spirit of the state that Allen described as a "nursery of hardy soldiers who would have a perfect detestation and abhorrence of arbitrary power." On many issues and across the political spectrum, modern Vermonters frequently invoke Allen's name in public discussion as proof that their positions represent the best of Vermont's traditions and values, and they still see in his thoughts expressions of the characteristics they like to attribute to their state.

History has recorded much of Ethan Allen's activities, but it remains far less clear how a son of the New England frontier became a prolific author whose words often reflected familiarity with both classical and contemporary intellectual currents. Allen's reputation rests primarily on his military exploits, especially the guerilla actions of the Green Mountain Boys and his bold capture of Fort Ticonderoga in May 1775 at the outset of the Revolutionary War. More typically he cowed his opponents with threats, humiliation, and bawled epithets; more than any participant in the long Yankee v. Yorker struggle for the area that became Vermont, he understood that "cunning and power are but the same thing." Ironically, Allen's only attempt to lead soldiers against a spirited opposition with trained and experienced leadership failed miserably. In the vanguard of the 1775 American thrust to add Canada to the thirteen rebelling colonies, his strategically and tactically flawed attempt to capture Montreal resulted in his capture. For most of the next three years, imprisonment and parole kept him out of action.

Resentful of his harsh treatment by the British, on his release in the spring of 1778 Allen formulated and wrote *A Narrative of Colonel Ethan Allen's Captivity,* published in Philadelphia in 1779 and republished several times within a few years. During the revolutionary era his *Narrative* reportedly outsold all other contemporary American publications, including Thomas Paine's *Common Sense.* Allen's capture of Fort Ticonderoga had launched him in the popular imagination well beyond Vermont, and the *Narrative* bolstered his reputation. In both the *Narrative* and throughout his life Ethan Allen exhibited a compulsive reflex to use strong, colorful, and often self-serving language. He assembled pen and paper, and forged them into potent weapons to protect Yankee speculators' and his neighbors' land claims against New York designs, to fight for American independence, or to assert and ensure the survival of Vermont independence.

Hints of the development of Allen's vivid rhetoric emerge in the story of his early life. He was born in Litchfield, Connecticut, in 1738, the first son of Joseph and Mary Allen. Possibly because of their leanings to the Anglican Church, very much a dissenting theology in Calvinist New England, Ethan's parents soon moved twenty-five miles northwest to the newly chartered town of Cornwall. Over the next eleven years, they presented Ethan with five brothers and two sisters, as they turned unsettled land into a large and productive farm. His new neighbors quickly recognized Joseph Allen as a leader, electing him to serve as a selectman and the moderator of Cornwall's first town meeting. Apparently intellectually alive and engaged, Joseph Allen may have stimulated his eldest son to emulate him.

Ethan Allen's biographers attribute the frequent relocations of the Allen family following their arrival in New England in 1632 to a "restless, energetic, hopeful" nature which impelled them to follow "the frontier persistently, clearing the wilderness, building cabins, and sowing crops which they often left for others to reap." The strong-willed Allens more likely chafed under the narrowness of puritan Massachusetts and later the orthodox Calvinism of the more settled parts of Connecticut. They probably moved to seek areas more congenial to their strongly held views of the nature of religion and society rather than from unbridled frontier wanderlust. In the 1630s, they followed Thomas Hooker, "a born democrat," to the Connecticut River valley. By the time Joseph Allen moved to Cornwall generations later, he had come to prefer the Church of England, professing the reformed Arminian theology that recognized the equality of all men in the sight of God rather than the prevailing Calvinist doctrine of absolute predetermination of the salvation of a select few.

Beginning in the 1730s, the Great Awakening championed by Jonathan Edwards from his Northampton, Massachusetts, pulpit spawned disputes within the Connecticut and other New England congregations that angered and threatened orthodox "Old Light"

Congregationalists. Propelled by the evangelical preaching of George Whitefield and his more democratic concept of the experience of "the New Birth," a self-validating event that gave everyone the hope of salvation, the "New Lights" and other separatist sects began to break away. In over 100 churches, about one-fourth of the organized parishes in New England, "New Light" adherents separated, forming new congregations. In many cases they migrated to the frontier and settled new towns like Cornwall. The Allens were part of this movement, and in the 1760s many of the early settlers in the Vermont area also came from the Connecticut and eastern New York regions of this separatist tradition to the New Hampshire Grants.

Despite the absence of a school in Cornwall, along with absorbing his father's thinking, Ethan read the Bible (probably the 1611 King James version) and Plutarch's *Lives* at home. When Ethan was sixteen, Joseph Allen sent his son to nearby Salisbury to prepare for Yale College under the tutelage of the Reverend Jonathan Lee. Here Ethan began the studies necessary for admission to Yale, originally formed as an Anglican institution in 1701 and deeply engaged in the major religious cross-currents of the mid-1700s. A 1742 graduate of Yale, Lee was "an animated and popular preacher" who "exerted an important influence in Connecticut churches" and sided with the "New Lights." Preparation for Yale in the 1750s would have centered on a curriculum that included classics ranging from Greek texts by Homer, Thucydides, Aristotle, Pindar, and Plato to such Roman authors as Juvenal, Cicero, Virgil, and Livius. It would also include arithmetic and Euclid's geometry, and Reverend Lee would probably have introduced his student to the more contemporary thought of Locke, Newton, Watts, and Dodsley as well.

How deeply young Ethan Allen traversed the work and ideas of any of these men in his few months with Reverend Lee remains unknown, for at the news of his father's death in early April 1755 Ethan abruptly left Salisbury and ended his studies. At the age of seventeen he returned to Cornwall to assume responsibility for the farm and his mother and siblings, but he did not allow the repetitive routine of the farm to deaden his curious and lively intellect. Farming, despite his success in adding to the family holdings in Cornwall, did not captivate Allen. At the age of nineteen in 1757 he served briefly with the militia during the French and Indian War. He also continued his late father's support of Reverend Palmer, who Joseph had converted to Anglicanism in 1754. The Congregational Church of Cornwall sued Palmer for breach of contract, and in 1761 Ethan, with his brother Heman and two others, wrote an "account of the usage of the Presbyterians towards the Church of England professors in Cornwall, written by desire of the Rev. Solomon Palmer."

In 1762, restless for something more than a life of farming, Ethan purchased a one-eighth interest in an ambitious iron-making operation in Salisbury, Connecticut. A year later he bought a small farm in Salisbury near the iron works and moved there with his bride Mary. In Salisbury Allen frequently drank and brawled, and he got into trouble with local authorities for defying the law and inoculating himself against smallpox. According to one later account, "Allen's managerial talent . . . fell far short of his entrepreneurial skills. In three tumultuous years ... he repeatedly demonstrated his physical prowess, shocked and (privately) entertained the townspeople with his rich command of profanity, and soon parted company with his partners."

If Ethan's Salisbury years did not advance his entrepreneurial ambitions, they did have a major impact on his intellectual and rhetorical development. At some point in his Salisbury residence Allen met Dr. Thomas Young, who lived a few miles away on the vast Livingston family estate in Armenia, New York. Six years Ethan's senior, Young had read voraciously as a child and had taught himself Latin, some Greek, French, and "a tolerable knowledge of German and Dutch." He would become, in John Adams' estimation, "a Firebrand, an Incendiary, an Eternal Fisher in Troubled Waters." "Boston," according to Adams, "will never be in peace while that fellow lives in it. He is a Scourge, a Pestilence, a Judgment." Young participated in the Boston Tea Party, observed the Boston Massacre, and dabbled in revolutionary activities in Rhode Island, New York, Pennsylvania, and possibly North Carolina. Benjamin Rush gave Young some credit for shaping Pennsylvania's radical 1776 state constitution, which Vermont employed for a pattern for its first constitution a year later. In 1777 Young urged Vermonters to set up their own government, and he has some claim on coining the term "Vermont." Ethan Allen apparently spent much time with Young and "fully imbibed all of his infidel notions."

In Armenia in the mid-1760s, Young, a skillful physician who later published well-regarded medical treatises, began to invest in land in what would become western Vermont through a highly speculative venture headed by John Henry Lydius. As his investment went sour, Young railed against "the great land-jobbers in New York." In his 1764 pamphlet on the issue, Young blamed the frustration of Lydius's claim on "envious monopolizing enemies" who thwarted the right of "the common people." Ignoring his speculative interest, the doctor argued for settlers who wanted to own land at "such rates as we can promise ourselves some recompense to our labours thereon." Ethan would later echo this language. According to one Allen biographer, Young probably discussed Locke, Hobbs, Machiavelli, Newton, Watts, Salmon on geography, and Charles Blount's 1693 deist manifesto *The Oracles of Reason* with his young friend as well.

Religion was a key component of Allen's intellectual relationship with Thomas Young. A confirmed deist charged with blasphemy in 1756 for declaring that "Jesus Christ was a knave and a fool," Young seems certain to have influenced Ethan's religious thinking. During their time together Young began to write "a lengthy, rambling essay, in which he drew upon his wide if undigested reading in science and philosophy." The essay remained unpublished, and in 1781 Allen retrieved the manuscript from Young's widow. Revising his friend's text and adding perhaps as much as another third to it, Ethan published it in 1784 as *Reason the Only Oracle of Man, or a Compenduous System of Natural Religion,* a ponderous title which quickly gave way in popular parlance to "Ethan Allen's Bible."

Thomas Young moved to Albany in 1764 to expedite his fight against Yorker authorities, and Allen's path never again intersected with the radical doctor. But in two short years Allen had eagerly drunk deeply from Young's well of radical political and philosophical ideas. In the years ahead Allen invoked many of the good doctor's ideas, just as he invoked biblical paraphrases and literary allusions to buttress his arguments and claims. Allen also began to speculate in Vermont land, purchasing New Hampshire titles in Vermont that New York authorities worked as hard to invalidate as they had the Lydius claims. Allen would react against New York officials just as strongly as Young had, and in the same vein.

In 1770 Allen burst on the scene in Vermont as the leader of the settlers, speculators, and proprietors holding New Hampshire titles in their legal battle against the claims of their New York counterparts. As he left Albany after losing in a New York court, Allen boldly warned New York Attorney General John Tabor Kempe to take care in dealing with the Yankees on the Grants. Adapting the Bible's 1 Kings 20:28 to drive home his point, Allen told Kempe, "The gods of the valleys are not Gods of the hills" and urged him to visit Bennington for clarification of his meaning.

From the time of these "ejectment suits," with the exception of his three years in captivity, through his words and deeds Ethan Allen became the most prominent Vermonter. In his rapidly growing volume of written work he cited some classical authors and biblical passages, but he more often used loose paraphrases to mold those references to his own purposes. Reporting to the New York Congress after capturing Fort Ticonderoga, he borrowed from Isaiah 40:31 to preach that

America "might rise on eagles' wings and mount up to glory, freedom and eternal honour." In the *Narrative* of his captivity Ethan drew from Matthew 4:8-9 to describe his rejection of a British attempt to turn him with an "offer of land to be similar to that which the devil offered Jesus Christ, 'To give him all the kingdoms of the world, if he would fall down and worship him.'" Later in the *Narrative* he adapted Thessalonians 2:11 to condemn General John Burgoyne and some other British officers with the strong line that "therefore God gave them over to strong delusions, to believe a lie, that they might be damned." If Allen more frequently paraphrased than he accurately quoted his Biblical and classical sources, given the raw power of the language he crafted it seems unlikely that many of his eighteenth-century readers or listeners shared John Tabor Kempe's puzzlement over his intent.

By the time Ethan exploded onto the Vermont stage, first assuming a leading regional role and then becoming one of the first national heroes of the American Revolution, he was already "much disposed to contemplation." As he later wrote, "At my commencement in manhood I committed to manuscript such sentiments or arguments as appeared most consonant with reason. . . . This method of scribbling I practiced for many years." He concluded that "as I was deficient in education . . . [I] had to acquire the knowledge of grammar and language as well as the art of reasoning, principally from a studious application to it." As the selections in this volume indicate, the results of this frontier self-education were remarkable. During the thirty-four years that remained to him after his father's death and leaving the instruction of

Reverend Lee, Ethan Allen's "scribblings" produced a body of forcefully composed letters, tracts, and books that make him the most quotable of all Vermonters.

Chronology

1738, JANUARY 10 – *Ethan Allen* born, Litchfield, Connecticut

1740 – Allen family moves to Cornwall, Connecticut

1755 – *Ethan Allen* begins preparation for Yale College with Rev. Lee in Salisbury, Connecticut

APRIL 14 – Death of *Ethan Allen's* father Joseph Allen, Cornwall, Connecticut; *Ethan Allen* returns to Cornwall to manage family farm

1762, JUNE 23 – *Ethan Allen* marries Mary Brownson, Woodbury, Connecticut

1762-64 – *Ethan Allen* involved with iron works, Salisbury, Connecticut, develops friendship with Dr. Thomas Young

1766-70 – *Ethan Allen* makes occasional visits to New Hampshire Grants (Vermont)

1770 – *Ethan Allen* becomes involved with Yankee investors in New Hampshire Grants real estate, represents them in court cases at Albany, New York; creation of the Green Mountain Boys to resist New York authority

1773, JANUARY – *Ethan Allen* and brothers, with cousin Remember Baker, form Onion River Land Company to invest in land in northwestern Vermont

1774 – New York passes "Bloody Act" outlawing *Ethan Allen* and associates; *Ethan Allen* publishes his *Brief Narrative*

1775, MAY 10 – *Ethan Allen* leads American force in capture of Fort Ticonderoga

SEPTEMBER 24 – *Ethan Allen* leads attack on Montreal, is captured by British

1777, JANUARY 15 – Convention at Westminster declares independence of "New Connecticut"

JULY – Convention at Windsor formalizes adoption of "Vermont" name, establishes framework for new government with the first state constitution

1778, MAY – *Ethan Allen* released from British captivity, returns to Vermont

AUGUST – *Ethan Allen* publishes *An Animadversory Address* on Vermont's right to remain independent

1779, MARCH – *Ethan Allen* completes writing of *A Narrative of Col. Ethan Allen's Captivity*

AUGUST – *Ethan Allen* publishes *A Vindication of the Opposition of the Inhabitants of Vermont to the Government of New York*

1780, JANUARY – *Ethan Allen* publishes *A Concise Refutation* with Jonas Fay

1780-81 – *Ethan Allen* and other Vermont leaders negotiate with Frederick Haldimand, commander of British forces in Canada, over possibility of Vermont's returning to British allegiance

1781 – *Ethan Allen* retrieves draft of *Reason the Only Oracle of Man* from Thomas Young's widow

1782, JANUARY – *Ethan Allen* publishes *The Present State of the Controversy*

JULY – *Ethan Allen* completes writing of *Reason the Only Oracle of Man*

1783, JUNE – death of Mary Brownson Allen

1784, FEBRUARY 9 –*Ethan Allen* marries Fanny Montresor Buchanan, Westminster, Vermont

1785, NOVEMBER – Printing completed on *Reason the Only Oracle of Man*

1786, SEPTEMBER – *Ethan Allen* travels to Wyoming Valley on behalf of settlers there engaged in dispute with Pennsylvania state government; publishes *An Address from the Inhabitants of Wyoming*

1787, MAY – *Ethan Allen* and family move from Sunderland, Vermont, to Burlington intervale farm that becomes the Ethan Allen Homestead

1788, JULY 16 – As part of Allen family opposition to growing movement toward statehood for Vermont, *Ethan Allen* solicits new trade and political relationship from Lord Dorchester, Governor-General of Canada

1789, FEBRUARY 12 – *Ethan Allen* dies on return trip from cousin Ebenezer Allen's farm in South Hero, Vermont

1791, JANUARY – Convention at Bennington votes in favor of Vermont joining the Union

MARCH 4 – Act of Congress welcoming Vermont as the fourteenth American state

The Quotable Ethan Allen

§

Ethan Allen trial for blasphemy, Salisbury, Connecticut, 1764

"By Jesus Christ, I wish I may be Bound Down in Hell with old Belzabub a Thousand Years in the Lowest Pitt in Hell and that Every Little Insipid Devil should come along and ask the Reason of Allens Lying there, [if] it Should be said [that] he made a promise . . . that he would have satisfaction of Lee and Stoddard and Did Not fulfill it."

§

Ethan Allen, Albany, New York, response to John Tabor Kempe's recruitment of him for New York, June 1770

"The gods of the valleys are not Gods of the hills."

§

Ethan Allen response to Charles Hutcheson, Yorker of Rupert, October 1771

"Go your way now, & complain to that damned Scoundrel your Governor. God damn your Governor, Laws, King, Council, & Assembly."

§

Ethan Allen in Connecticut Courant, March 24, 1772

"Can the New York scribblers . . . alter wrong into right, or make any person of good sense believe that a great number of hard labouring peasants, going through the fatigues of settlement, and cultivation of a howling wilderness, are a community of riotous, disorderly, licentious, treasonable persons?"

❧

Ethan Allen, Bennington, to Benjamin Spencer et al., January 11, 1774

"On my return from that You Call the Mobb I was Consernd for Your Wellfare Fearing that the force of our arms would Urge You to purchaise Newhampshire Title at an Unreasonable rate, tho, at the same Time I Know Not but that after the force is withdrawn You will want a Third army."

❧

Ethan Allen and Remember Baker to "the Inhabitants of Clarendon," January 13, 1774

"I abhor to put a staff into the hands of Colvin or any other rascal to defraud your settlers. The Hampshire title must, nay shall, be had for all settlers as are in quest of it, at a reasonable rate, nor shall any villain by a sudden purchase impose on old settlers."

"I assure you it is not the design of our mobs to betray you into the hands of villainous purchasers. None but blockheads would purchase your farms and must be treated as such."

❧

Ethan Allen, Bennington, to Crean Brush & Samuel Wells, May 19, 1774

"You are but busie Understrappers to a Number of more Overgrown Villains which Can Murther by Law without remorse. I Have to Inform that the Green Mountain Boys will Not Tamely resign their necks to the Halter to be Hanged by Your Curst Fraternity of Land

Jockeys who Would Better Adorn a halter than we, therefore as You regard Your Own Lives be Carefull Not to Invade ours for what Measure you Meat it shall be Measured to You Again."

"As a Testimony of Gratitude for the many unmerited Kindnesses, and services, you have Done us the last Sessions at New York &c &c we Intend Shortly visiting your Abode, Where we hope to have the Honour of Presenting you with the BEECH SEAL:—which we Beg your kind Acceptance off, as a mark of the high Esteem we have of your Person and as a Token of our Approbation for the Eminent Exertions you Displayed of your Abilitys in Bringing about the Salutary act of the 9th of March last."

§

Ethan Allen, Bennington, to Theodore Atkinson, November 15, 1774

"If it Shall Appear I have failed in my Design I am Conscious my Intention was Good and for the future Shall Not Trouble Your honour or the Publick with my Scribling but shall 'Drop into my Self and be a fool.'"

§

A Brief Narrative of the Proceedings of the Government of New-York, Relative to Their Obtaining the Jurisdiction of That Large District of Land, to the Westward from Connecticut River (1774)

"If the New-York Patentees will remove their Patents that have been subsequently lapped and laid on the New-Hampshire Charters, and quiet us in our Possessions, agreeable to his Majesty's directions, and suspend those criminal Prosecutions against us for being Rioters (as we are unjustly denominated) then will our Settlers be orderly and submissive subjects to Government; but be it known to that despotic Fraternity of Law-Makers and Law-Breakers, that we will not be fooled or frighted out of our Property; they have broke over his Majesty's express Prohibitions, in patenting those Lands, and when they act in conformity to the regal Authority of Great-Britain, it will be soon enough for us to obey them."

"The Emblems of their insatiable, avaricious, overbearing, inhuman, barbarous, and blood-guiltiness of Disposition and Intention is therein portraited in that transparent Image of themselves, which cannot fail to be a Blot, and an infamous Reproach to them, to Posterity."

"Their Tenants groan under their Usury and Oppression; and they have gained, as well as merited the Disapprobation and Abhorrence of their Neighbours, and the innocent Blood they have already shed, calls for Heaven's Vengeance on their guilty Heads; and if they should come forth in arms against us, thousands of their injured and dissatisfied Neighbours in the several Governments, will join with us, to cut off, and extirpate such an execrable Race from the Face of the Earth!"

"In fine, every Opposition to their monarchical Government is deemed Felony, and at the End of every such Sentence, there is the Word DEATH!"

"Those bloody Law-Givers know we are necessitated to oppose their Execution of Law, where it points directly at our Property, or give up the same: But there is one Thing is Matter of Consolation to us, viz. that printed Sentences of Death will not kill us when we are at a Distance; and if the Executioners approach us, they will be as likely to fall Victims to Death as we: And that Person, or Country of Persons, are Cowards indeed, if they cannot as manfully fight for their Liberty, Property and Life, as Villains can do to deprive them thereof."

"And we flatter ourselves, upon Occasion, we can muster as good a Regiment of Mark's-men and Scalpers, as America can afford; and we now give . . . all the Land-Jobbers of New-York, an Invitation to come and view the Dexterity of our Regiment; and we cannot think of a better Time for that Purpose, than when the Executioners come to kill us, by Virtue of the Authority their Judges have lately received to award and Sentence us to Death in our Absence."

"Draco, the Athenian Lawgiver, caused a Number of Laws (in many Respects analogous to those we have been speaking of) to be written in Blood. But our modern Draco's determine to have their's verified in Blood. They well know we shall more than Three, nay, more than Three Times Three Hundred, assemble together, if Need be, to maintain our common Cause."

"People in general cannot but be sensible that the Title of our Land is in Reality the Bone of Contention; and that as a People, we behave ourselves orderly; and are industrious, and honestly disposed; and pay just Deference to Order and good Government; and that we mean no more by that which is called the MOB, but to defend our just Rights and Properties."

"We will kill and destroy any Person or Persons whomsoever, that shall presume to be accessory, aiding or assisting in taking any of us as aforesaid; for by these Presents we give any such disposed Person or Persons to understand, that, altho' they have a License by the Law aforesaid, to kill us; and an 'Indemnification' for such Murther from the same Authority; yet they have no Indemnification for so doing, from the GREEN MOUNTAIN BOYS."

"But if the Governmental Authority of New-York will Judge in their own Case, and act in Opposition to that of Great-Britain, and insist upon killing us to take possession of our 'Vine-yards' come on, we are ready for a Game of Scalping with them; for our martial Spirits glow with Bitter Indignation, and consummate Fury, to Blast their Infernal Projections."

"We are under Necessity of resisting, even unto Blood, every Person who may attempt to take us as Felons or Rioters aforesaid; for in this Case it is not resisting Law, but only opposing Force by Force."

"Laws and Society-compacts, were made to protect and secure the Subjects in their peaceable Possessions and Properties, and not to subvert them. No Person or Community of Persons can be supposed to be under any particular Compact or Law, except it presupposeth, that that Law will protect such Persons or Community of Persons in his or their Properties, for otherways the Subject would by Law be bound to be accessory to his own Ruin and Destruction, which is inconsistent with the Law of Self-preservation; but this Law being natural as well as eternal, can never be abrogated by the Law of Men."

"If we do not oppose the Sheriff and his Possy, he takes immediate Possession of our Houses and Farms, if we do, we are immediately indicted Rioters; and when others oppose Officers in taking such their Friends so indicted, they are also indicted and so on, there being no End of Indictment against us so long as we Act the bold and manly Part, and stand by our Liberty."

"Right and Wrong, are eternally the same to all Periods of Time, Places and Nations, and colouring a Crime with a specious Pretence of Law, only adds to the Criminality of it; for it subverts the very Design of Law, prostituting it to the vilest Purposes."

"Our Breasts glow with a martial Fury to defend our Persons and Fortunes from the Ravages of those that would Destroy us."

"Such Hypocrisy debases Human Nature, is the Pest of Society, partakes of Falshood and Treachery; and what renders it peculiarly vile is that it usurps the Seat of Virtue, and destroys Faith in Communities, and is the Source of cruel Jealousy."

"When Laws in their original Design and Administration, are degenerated from the good Ends for which Laws and Government were Instituted, terminating in the Ruin and Destruction of the Society it should secure and protect, from the same Principles, viz. Self-preservation, the Subjects are obliged to resist and depose such Government."

"They have erected several Companies, which by the Votes of the Soldiers are furnished with Officers; these Companies form a Regiment which are known by the significant Character of GREEN MOUNTAIN BOYS, who are generally in the Prime of Life, well versed in the Use of Fire-Arms, and of robust Constitutions; probably no American Regiment in an interior Defence could excel them."

❧

Ethan Allen, Sheffield, Massachusetts, to Oliver Wolcott, March 1, 1775

"Provided the Controversy between Great Britain and the Colonies Should Terminate in a War the Regiment of Green Mountain Boys Will I Dare Ingage to Assist their American Brethren in the Capacity of Rangers."

❧

Ethan Allen, Fort Ticonderoga, to the Albany Committee of Correspondence, May 11, 1775

"I Have the Inexpressible Satisfaction to Acquaint you that at Day break of the Eleventh Instant (Pursuant to my Directions from Sundry Leading Gentlemen in the Colonies of Massachusetts Bay and Connecticut) I Took the Fortress of Ticonderoga with About one Hundred and thirty Green Mountain Boys."

❧

Ethan Allen, Fort Ticonderoga, to the Massachusetts Congress, May 11, 1775

"The soldiery behaved with such resistless fury, that they so terrified the King's Troops that they durst not fire on their assailants, and our soldiery was agreeably disappointed."

ETHAN ALLEN'S

NARRATIVE

OF THE CAPTURE OF

TICONDEROGA,

AND OF

His Captivity and Treatment by the British.

WRITTEN BY HIMSELF.

FIFTH EDITION, WITH NOTES.

BURLINGTON:
C. GOODRICH & S. B. NICHOLS.
WICKWARE BUILDING.

1849.
C.

§

Ethan Allen, Fort Ticonderoga, to Jonathan Trumbull, May 12, 1775

"I make You a Present of a Major a Captain and Two Lieuts in the regular Establishment of George the Third."

"I Hope in a Short Time to be Authorized to acquaint Your Honour that Lake Champlain & the fortifications thereon are subjected to the Colonies. The Enterprise has been approbated by the Officers and Soldiary of the Green Mountain Boys. Nor do I hesitate as to the Success."

§

Ethan Allen, Fort Ticonderoga, to the Albany Committee of Safety, May 12, 1775

"As we are In Want of Almost Every Necessary (Courage Excepted) We Earnestly Request your Immediate Relief, By Troops, Provision, Arms and Ammunition."

§

Ethan Allen, St. Johns, Canada, to "Mr. James Morrison and the Marchants that are friendly to the Cause of Liberty in Montreal," May 18, 1775

"I Have the pleasure to Acquaint You that Lake George & Champlain with the Fortresses Artillery &c particularly the armed Sloop of George the Third with all Water Carrages on Those Lakes are Now in the Possession of the Colonies."

§

Ethan Allen, Fort Ticonderoga, to Noah Lee, May 21, 1775

"We met with a Canonading of Grape Shot. The Musick was both Terrible and Delightfull."

§

Ethan Allen, Crown Point, to "the several Tribes of Indians in Canada," May 24, 1775

"As King George's soldiers Killed our Brothers and Friends in a Time of Peace I hope as Indians are Good and Honest men You will Not fight for King George Against Your Friends in America as they have Done You no wrong and Desire to Live with You as Brothers."

"I was Always a Friend to Indians and have Hunted with them many Times and Know how to Shoot and Ambush Like Indians and am a Great Hunter."

"I will Go with You Into the woods to Scout and my men and Your men will sleep Together and Eat and Drink Together and fight regulars because they first Killed our Brothers and will fight against us therefore I want our Brother Indians to Help us fight for I know Indians are good warriers and Can fight well in the Bush."

§

Ethan Allen, Fort Ticonderoga, to Noah Lee, May 25, 1775

"I Expect Shortly the Continental Congress will Appoint a Comander for this Department so that You Need Not Hold Your preferment Either Under the Core of G M Boys or Col. Arnold. Undoubtedly we Shall all be rewarded According to our Merit in this or the Coming world."

❧

Ethan Allen, Crown Point, to the Continental Congress, May 29, 1775

"Provided they should after all their Good Service in behalf of their Country be Neglected and Left Exposed they will be of all men the most Consummately miserable."

"The Canadians all Except the Nobliss and also the Indians apear at Present to be Very friendly to us, and it is my Humble Opinion that the more Vigurous the Colonies Push the war against the Kings Troops in Canada the more friends we shall find in that Country. Provided I had but five hundred men with me at St. Johns when we Took the Kings Sloop I would have advanced to Montreal."

"They are a Set of Gentlemen that will Not be Converted by reason but are Easily wrought upon by fear."

"It is bad policy to fear the resentment of an Enemy."

"There are many Advantages in forming the frontier Near the Country of the Enemy as first it will be in our Power to ravage and make Inroads into the Heart of the Enemies Country the same as they might Easily Do were they in Possession and Command of Lake Champlain."

❧

Ethan Allen, Crown Point, to the New York Congress, June 2, 1775

"I wish to God *America* would, at this critical juncture, exert herself agreeable to the indignity offered her by a tyrannical Ministry. She might rise on eagles' wings, and mount up to glory, freedom, and immortal honour, if she did but know and exert her strength. Fame is now hovering over her head. A vast Continent must now sink to slavery, poverty, horrour, and bondage, or rise to unconquerable freedom, immense wealth, inexpressible felicity, and immortal fame."

"I will lay my life on it, that with fifteen hundred men and a proper train of artillery, I will take *Montreal.* Provided I could be thus furnished, and if an Army could command the field, it would be no insuperable difficulty to take *Quebeck.*"

"It is as long as it is broad, the more that are sent to *Quebeck,* the less they [England] can send to *Boston,* or any other part of the continent."

"The thing that so unites the temper of the *Indians* to us, is our taking the sovereignty of Lake *Champlain.* They have wit enough to make a good bargain, and stand by the strongest side."

"Cunning and power are but the same thing . . . but cunning without power can hold no equal contest with that which is armed with it."

❧

Ethan Allen, Fort Ticonderoga, to "the Canadians," June 4, 1775

"One story is good until another is told."

"Pray let old England and the Colonies fight it out; and you Canadians, stand by and see what an arm of flesh can do."

§

Ethan Allen, Bennington, to Jonathan Trumbull, July 12, 1775

"I Lay my Honour on it that the Indians in General I might almost have Said the same of the Canadians are Disposed to be Either Nuters or Assistants to the United Colonies."

"Were it Not that the Grand Continental Congress had Lately Incorporated the Green Mountain Boys into a Battallion Under Certain regulation and Command I would fourthwith Advance them Into Canada and Invest Montreal Exclusive of any help from the Colonies."

"I would Not for my Right arm act without or Contrary to Orders. If my Fond Zeal of Reducing the Kings Fortresses and Destroying or Imprisoning his Troops in Canada be the Result of Enthusiasm I Hope and Expect the wisdom of the Continent will Treat it as Such and on the other hand if it Proceed from Sound Policy that the Plan will be Adopted."

§

Ethan Allen, Fort Ticonderoga, to the New York Congress, July 20, 1775

"I hope no gentlemen in the Congress will retain any preconceived prejudices against me, as, on my part, I shall not against any of them; but as soon as opportunity may permit and the publick cause not suffer thereby, shall hold myself in readiness to settle all former disputes and grievances on honourable terms."

❧

Ethan Allen, Fort Ticonderoga, to Jonathan Trumbull, August 3, 1775

"Notwithstanding my zeal and success in my Country's cause, the old farmers on the *New-Hampshire Grants,* who do not incline to go to war, have met in a Committee meeting, and in their nomination of officers for the Regiment of *Green Mountain Boys* who are quickly to be raised, have wholly omitted me."

"I find myself in the favour of the officers of the Army and the young *Green Mountain Boys.* How the old men came to reject me, I cannot conceive, inasmuch as I saved them from the encroachments of *New-York.*"

❧

Ethan Allen, "near Chambly," Canada, to Philip Schuyler & Richard Montgomery, September 8, 1775

"We are Told the Indians Murmer Against the regulars on Account of their Slain as they urged them Into the war, the more You Kill of them the Better, Exchange of Life for Toys they find to be unequal."

❧

Ethan Allen, St. Ours, Canada, to Richard Montgomery, September 20, 1775

"Those that used to be enemies to our cause come cap in hand to me; and I swear by the Lord I can raise three times the number of our Army in Canada, provided you continue the siege; it all depends on that."

"The glory of a victory which will be attended with such important consequences, will crown all our fatigues, risks, and labours; to fail of victory will be an eternal disgrace, but to obtain it will elevate us on the wings of fame."

❦

Ethan Allen, Montreal, Canada, to Richard Prescott, September 25, 1775

"In the wheel of transitory events, I find myself prisoner, and in irons."

❦

Ethan Allen, Cork, Ireland, to "the Gentlemen of Cork," January 24, 1776

"I received your generous present this day with a joyful heart. Thanks to God there are still the feelings of humanity in the worthy citizens of Cork towards those of their bone and flesh, who, through misfortune from the present broils in the empire are needy prisoners."

❦

Ethan Allen, Halifax, Canada, to the Connecticut Assembly, August 12, 1776

"I assure you that the English rascally treatment to me has wholly erased my former feelings of parent State, mother country, and, in fine, all kindred and friendly connexion with them. . . . If I must suffer the vengeance and ignominy of tyrants, it would be more graceful from Turks, Moors, and barbarians."

❧

Ethan Allen, Long Island, New York, to the Connecticut Assembly, April 30, 1777

"Altho, this Mode of Existance is Very urksome, yet it is not deplorable, by reason of hope, the Officers on parole seam to be mere Ciphers, Exempted from both danger and honour, resless man Indeed will never be Easie in any circumstances whatever, but it is Extreamly Painfull to a Generous and Enterprising mind, to be thus debard from Sharing the Glories, that are to be Revealed in the course of this Campain, the Officers must generally Lament the Appearance of their Continued fate."

❧

Ethan Allen, Long Island, New York, to the Massachusetts Board of War, July 19, 1777

"You will not be surprised that I express some anxious desire for the possession of Liberty which I have been stranger to for near two years."

❧

Ethan Allen, Long Island, New York, to Levi Allen, July 27, 1777

"I do hereby certify you that I have wholly recovered my constitution; have a clear exercise of reason, and enjoy a philosophical serenity of mind under the circumstances of imprisonment."

"The death of my little boy closely affected the tender passions of my soul, and by turn gives me the most sensible grief."

❧

Ethan Allen, Valley Forge, to Henry Laurens, May 9, 1778

"The Melevolent Cruelty Inflicted on me by the British in the Course of my Captivity is Scarcely to be Paralled in History."

❧

Ethan Allen, Bennington, to John Stark, May 12, 1778

"The tories & friends of tories give us some trouble yet; they contribute to the anarchy which now reigns among us, and I am of the opinion that We shall never be at peace, while one of them is suffered to remain in the country."

❧

Ethan Allen, Bennington, to Henry Laurens, June 17, 1778

"The Green Mountain Boys have never failed to give the Enemy a Trimming, when Ever they have Come together, War has become the Science of this People, and I flatter my Self, that the Congress have as loyal Subjects in these parts, as in any District, of America."

❧

Ethan Allen, Arlington, to Elisha Payne, July 11, 1778

"Cumberland County is greatly infested with New York Malcontents."

§

Ethan Allen, Albany, New York, to Horatio Gates, July 15, 1778

"I Have to add that I am now in a State of Perfect health, and ready to Serve my Country in the field, Provide a Person of my abilities should be wanted, Tho' I have plenty of Business of my own, and it is probable to me, that you have Plenty of Officers."

§

An Animadversory Address to the Inhabitants of the State of Vermont (1778)

"Many times I have hazarded my life for you, as well as for my own property; and if occasion shall in future require, will freely do it again."

"The New York patentees got judgement against those under New-Hampshire at trials at common law; but the claimants under New-Hampshire appealed to club law, and in this mode of trial, they beat the claimants under New-York."

"All good and wise men, will exert themselves in establishing and supporting good government and order, which are inseparably connected together."

"I was called by the Yorkers an outlaw, and afterwards by the British was called a rebel; and I humbly conceive, that there was as much propriety in the one name as the other, and I verily believe, that the King's Commissioners would now be as willing to pardon me for the sin of rebellion, provided I would afterwards be a subject to Britain, as the Legislature abovementioned, provided I would be a subject to New-York; and, I must confess, I had as leave be a subject to the one as the other; and, it is well known, I have had great experience with them both."

"In your early struggles with that government [New York] you acquired a reputation of bravery; this gave you a relish for martial glory, and the British invasion opened an ample field for its display, and you have gone on conquering and to conquer until tall grenadiers are dismayed and tremble at your approach. Your frontier situation often obliges you to be in arms and battles; and by repeated marchings, scoutings and manly exercises, your nerves have become strong to strike the mortal blow. What enemy to the state of Vermont, or New-York land monopolizer, shall be able to stand before you in the day of your fierce anger!"

Ethan Allen, Bennington, to George Washington, March 1, 1779

"Undoubtedly your Excellency will readily conceive that this part of the Country have done more than their adequate proportion in the war, and tho' they are greatly reduced as to materials to maintain standing forces, yet on sudden emergences the Militia is able and willing to face any equal number of the Enemy provided they should have no other reward but the Satisfaction of defeating them."

§

Ethan Allen, Bennington, to Meshech Weare, March 4, 1779

"I have this further reason for the Exertion of Government, as I am confident that Argument will be lost with them for the heads of the Schism at large, are a Petulent, Pettifoging, Scribling sort of Gentry, that will keep any Government in hot water till they are Thoroughly brought under, by the Exertions of authority."

§

Ethan Allen, Westminster, at trial of Eastside Yorkers, Spring 1779

"With my logic and reasoning from the eternal fitness of things I can upset your Blackstones, your whitestones, your gravestones, and your brimstones."

§

A Vindication of the Opposition of the Inhabitants of Vermont to the Government of New-York, and of Their Right to Form an Independent State (1779)

"Is it not altogether probable, that those inhabitants who have suffered so much from Yorkish and British tyranny, will yet take the field against the government of New-York, (if need be) and at the muzzle of their firelocks convince them of the independency of the state of Vermont; and that their said patents are no more than an intrusion on the right of the green Mountain boys."

"There were a number of depraved and mean spirited rascals which bit at the bait, and would probably have assisted that designing government of land clenchers, to divide the people, and finally inslaved them, had not the integrity and heroism of the green mountain boys prevented it, making it dangerous for any to except such commission, or secure his farm on the ruin of his neighbours."

"At the time the government of New-York confederated with the other states, the inhabitants of Vermont had formed their constitution, elected their chief, and other magistrates, and were in full possession of government; and as they were free and unconnected with any state or body politic, had a just right to do so. This right they received from nature, nor were they beholden to the government of New-York or any other power short of the omnipotent."

"There appears to be a great degree of similarity in this controversy with the British government with that of Vermont against the government of New-York, except in this respect, that the territory of Vermont was never under the jurisdiction of New-York."

"The detestable acts of outlawry passed the 9th day of March 1774, by the legislative authority of the colony of New-York, particularly against the inhabitants of Vermont was, in substance, a positive declaration of war against them."

"Thus the inhabitants ... were obliged either to give up their inheritance, or in the Yorkish sense of the word become outlaws, fellons, rioters, &c. and be subjected to the dangers and hazards of the shocking evils before mentioned, which nothing but the daring spirit and unconquerable fortitude of the green mountain boys prevented taking place."

"The people of Vermont consider themselves as being virtually in union with the united states, from the time that they took possession of lake Champlain, and the garrisons depending thereon, in behalf of the united states, in May 1775; from which early period of the revolution, they have taken an active part with them, and have pursued invariable, the same object, viz. liberty; have participated in all their troubles; and with them have hazarded all that is worth living or dying for."

"What a nursery of hardy soldiers may in future be nourished and supported in this fertile country ... stimulated with the spirit of liberty, having a perfect detestation and abhorrence of arbitrary power; from the exertions whereof they have suffered so much evil; will instill the principles of liberty and social virtue in their children, which will be perpetuated to future generations; their climate and interior remove from the sea coast, will naturally be productive of a laborious life, by which means they will be in great measure exempted from luxury and effeminacy, and be a valuable support to the rising empire of the new world."

❧

A Narrative of Col. Ethan Allen's Captivity (1779)

"Ever since I arrived to a state of manhood, and acquainted myself with the general history of mankind, I have felt a sincere passion for liberty."

"Friends and fellow-soldiers, you have, for a number of years past, been a scourge and terror to arbitrary power. Your valour has been famed abroad, and acknowledged, as appears by the advice and orders to me (from the General Assembly of Connecticut) to surprise and take the garrison now before us. I now propose to advance before you, and in person conduct you through the wicket-gate; for we must this morning either quit our pretensions to valour, or possess ourselves of this fortress in a few minutes; and, in as much as it is a desperate attempt, (which none but the bravest of men dare undertake) I do not urge it on any contrary to his will. You that will undertake voluntarily, poise your firelocks."

"I answered him, 'In the name of the great Jehovah, and the Continental Congress.'"

"This surprise was carried into execution in the gray of the morning of the 10th day of May, 1775. The sun seemed to rise that morning with a superior lustre; and Ticonderoga and its dependencies smiled on its conquerors, who tossed about the flowing bowl, and wished success to Congress, and the liberty and freedom of America."

"I had previously chosen my ground, but when I saw the number of the enemy, as they sallied out of the town, I perceived it would be a day of trouble, if not of rebuke."

"Then he shook his cane over my head, calling me many hard names, among which he frequently used the word rebel, and put himself in a great rage. I told him he would do well not to cane me, for I was not accustomed to it, and shook my fist at him, telling him that that was the beetle of mortality for him, if he presumed to strike."

"I therefore stepped between the executioners and the Canadians, opened my cloaths, and told gen. Prescott to thrust his bayonets into my breast, for I was the sole cause of the Canadians taking up arms."

"To give an instance upon being insulted, in a fit of anger I twisted off a nail with my teeth, which I took to be a ten-penny nail; it went through the mortise of the bar of my hand-cuff... I heard one say, damn him, can he eat iron?"

"The reader will readily conceive I was anxious about my preservation, (knowing that I was in the power of a haughty and cruel nation, considered as such.) Therefore the first proposition which I determined in my own mind was, that humanity and moral suasion would not be consulted in the determining of my fate: And those that daily came in great numbers, out of curiosity to see me, both gentle and simple, united in this, that I would be hanged. A gentlemen from America, by the name of Temple, (and who was friendly to me) just whispered me in the ear, and told me, that bets were laid in London, that I would be executed."

"This gave me inward satisfaction, (though I carefully concealed it with a pretended resentment) for I found I had come Yankee over him, and that the letter had gone to the identical person I designed it for."

"I lastly determined, (in my own mind) that if a cruel death must inevitably be my portion, I would face it undaunted, and tho' I greatly rejoice that I have returned to my country and friends, and to see the power and pride of Great Britain humbled; yet I am confident I could (then) die without the least appearance of dismay."

"The cause I was engaged in, I ever viewed worthy hazarding my life for, nor was I (at the most critical moments of trouble) sorry that I engaged in it; and as to the world of spirits, though I knew nothing of the mode or manner of it, expected nevertheless, when I should arrive at such a world, that I should be as well treated as other gentlemen of my merit."

"I gave for answer, that I chose freedom in every sense of the word: Then one of them asked me, what my occupation in life had been? I answered him, that in my younger days I had studied divinity, but was a conjurer by profession. He replied, that I conjured wrong at the time that I was taken; and I was obliged to own, that I mistook a figure at that time, but that I conjured them out of Ticonderoga. This was a place of great notoriety in England, so that the joke seemed to go in my favour."

"Two clergymen came to see me, and inasmuch as they behaved with civility, I returned them the same: We discoursed on several parts of moral philosophy and christianity; and they seemed to be surprised, that I should be acquainted with such topics, or that I should understand a syllogism or regular mode of argumentation. I am apprehensive my Canadian dress contributed not a little to the surprise, and excitement of curiosity: To see a gentleman in England, regularly dressed and well behaved, would be no sight at all; but such a rebel, as they were pleased to call me, it is probable was never before seen in England."

"The captain replied, that he needed no directions of mine how to treat a rebel; that the British would conquer the American rebels, hang the Congress, and such as promoted the rebellion, (me in particular) and retake their own prisoners; so that my life was of no consequence in the scale of their policy. I gave him for answer, that if they stayed 'till they conquered America, before they hanged me, I should die of old age."

"I then endeavoured to touch his humanity, but found he had none; for his prepossession of bigotry to his own party, had confirmed him in an opinion, that no humanity was due to unroyalists, but seemed to think that heaven and earth were made merely to gratify the king and his creatures; he uttered considerable unintelligible and groveling ideas, a little tinctured with monarchy, but stood well to his text of hanging me."

"Sometimes in the first week of June, we came to anchor at the Hook off New-York, where we remained but three days; in which time governor Tryon, Mr. Kemp, the old attorney general of New York, and several other perfidious and over-grown tories and land-jobbers, came on board. Tryon viewed me with a stern countenance … but never spoke to me, though it is altogether probable that he thought of the old quarrel between him, the old government of New-York, and the Green Mountain Boys."

"At another sitting he offered to bet a dozen of wine, that fort Washington would be in the hands of the British in three days. I stood the bet … and that day the fort was taken sure enough. Some months after, (when I was on parole) he called upon me with his usual humor, and mentioned the bet. I acknowledged I had lost it, but he said he did not mean to take it then, as I was a prisoner; that he would another day call on me, when their army came to Bennington. I replied that he was quite too generous, as I had fairly lost it; beside the Green

Mountain Boys would not suffer them to come to Bennington. This was all in good humour. I should have been glad to have seen him after the defeat at Bennington, but did not."

"My constitution was almost worn out by such a long and barbarous captivity. The enemy gave out that I was crazy, and wholly unmanned, but my vitals held sound, (nor was I delirious any more than I have been from my youth up; but my extreme circumstances at certain times, rendered it political to act in some measure the madman) and in consequence of a regular diet and exercise, my blood recruited, and my nerves in great measure recovered their former tone, strength and usefulness, in the course of six months."

"After I had examined more particularly into their truly deplorable condition, and had become more fully apprised of the essential facts, I was persuaded that it was a premeditated and systematical plan of the British council, to destroy the youths of our land, with a view thereby to deter the country, and make it submit to their despotism."

"I readily grant that instances of public virtue are no excitement to the sordid and vicious, nor on the other hand, will all the barbarity of Britain and Heshland awaken them to a sense of their duty to the public; but these things will have their proper effect on the generous and the brave."

"I then replied, 'That if by faithfulness I had recommended myself to gen. Howe, I should be loth, by unfaithfulness, to lose the general's good opinion; besides, that I viewed the offer of land to be similar to that which the devil offered Jesus Christ, "To give him all the kingdoms of the world, if he would fall down and worship him;" when at the same time that the damned soul had not one foot of land upon earth.'"

"Burgoyne was their toast and demi god: To him they paid adoration: In him the tories placed their confidence, 'and forgot the Lord their God,' and served Howe, Burgoyne, and Knyphausen, 'and became vile in their own imaginations, and their foolish hearts were darkened, professing' to be great politicians, and relying on foreign and merciless invaders, and with them seeking the ruin, bloodshed and destruction of their country, 'became fools,' expecting with them to share a dividend in the confiscated estates of their neighbours and countrymen, who fought for the whole country, and the religion and liberties thereof: — 'Therefore God gave them over to strong delusions, to believe a lie, that they all might be damned.'"

"This [Joshua] Loring is a monster! ... He is the most mean-spirited, cowardly, deceitful, and destructive animal in God's creation below, and legions of infernal devils, with all their tremendous horrors, are impatiently ready to receive [General] Howe and him, with all their detestable accomplices, into the most exquisite agonies of the hottest region of hell-fire."

"This plan being adopted by the general and his council of war, the little militia brigade of undisciplined heroes, with their long brown firelocks, (the best security of a free people) without either cannon or bayonets, was, on the 16th day of August, led on to the attack by their bold commanders in the face of the enemy's dreadful fire, (and to the astonishment of the world, and burlesque of discipline) carried every part of their lines in less than one quarter of an hour after the attack became general, took their cannon, killed and captivated more than two thirds of their number, which immortalized general Stark, and made Bennington famous to posterity."

"I wish my countrymen in general could but have an idea of the assuming tyranny, and haughty, malevolent, and insolent behavour of the enemy at that time [August 1777]; and from thence discern the intolerable calamities which this country have extricated themselves from by their public spiritedness and bravery."

"The downfall of general Burgoyne, and surrender of his army, dashed the aspiring hopes and expectations of the enemy, and brought low the imperious spirit of an opulent, puissant and haughty nation, and made the tories bite the ground with anguish, exalted the valour of the free-born sons of America, and raised their fame and that of their brave commanders to the clouds, and immortalized general Gates with laurels of eternal duration."

"Vaunt no more Old England! consider you are but an island! and that your power had been continued longer than the exercise of your humanity. Order your broken and vanquished battalions to retire from America, the scene of your cruelties. Go home and repent in dust and sackcloth for your aggravated crimes. The cries of bereaved parents, widows, and orphans, reach the Heavens, and you are abominated by every friend to America. Take your friends the tories with you, and be gone, and drink deep the cup of humiliation."

"I have something of a smattering of philosophy, and understand human nature in all its stages tolerably well; am thoroughly acquainted with your national crimes, and assure you that they not only cry aloud for Heaven's vengeance, but excite mankind to rise up against you."

"My affections are frenchified. – I glory in Louis the sixteenth, the generous and powerful ally of these states; am fond of a connection with so enterprising, learned, polite, courteous, and commercial a nation, and am sure that I express the sentiments and feelings of all the friends to the present revolution. I begin to learn the French tongue, and recommend it to my countrymen before Hebrew, Greek or Latin."

"I then bid farewell to my noble general [Washington] and the gentlemen of his retinue, and set out for Bennington, the capital of the Green Mountain Boys, where I arrived the evening of the last day of May to their great surprise; for I was to them as rose from the dead, and now both their joy and mine was complete. Three cannon were fired that evening, and next morning colonel Herrick gave orders, and fourteen more were discharged, welcoming me to Bennington, my usual place of abode; thirteen for the United States, and one for young Vermont."

"After this ceremony was ended we moved the flowing bowl, and rural felicity, sweetened with friendship, glowed in each countenance, and with loyal healths to the rising State of America, concluded that evening, and with the same loyal spirit, I now conclude my narrative."

❧

Ethan Allen, Sunderland, to Christopher Carleton, November 24, 1780

"I fully agree with his Excellency General Halderman, that the present Cartel respects Vermont, exclusive of any Connections whatever with the United States, with whom this State are wholly unconnected, and who are, and for a long Time have been in a Spirited Controversy with the State of New York."

❧

Ethan Allen, Sunderland, to John Stark, December 7, 1780

"The transactions of this State in making a truce with the British and bringing forward a Cartel for the exchange of Prisoners has considerably engrossed the attention of the public. . . . I expect a manifesto will be published in which will be Exhibited many things which the public are anxious to know. Till that time people must be content with such Conjectures as best suits.—I am at a loss to form an Idea what the people of the United States would have Vermont to do."

❧

A Concise Refutation of the Claims of New-Hampshire and Massachusetts-Bay to the Territory of Vermont (with Jonas Fay) (1780)

"This government, astonished at the late extraordinary claims of New-Hampshire and Massachusetts-Bay to the territory of Vermont, and the following remarks having been omitted in any piece heretofore published on the subject, find themselves under the disagreeable necessity of publicly exposing the imbecility, and depravity of those governments, whose candour, on the very first attempt, should have suggested to them, that in prosecuting such claims, they would unavoidably become accomplices with the government of New-York, in their many aggravated and long continued oppressions of the people of this State."

"The claim of New-York therefore only survived that of New-Hampshire from the arbitrary decree of 1764, to the glorious aera of American Liberty and Independence, which was declared the fourth day of July 1776, and then expired also, to the inexpressible joy of the free citizens of Vermont, who, in consequence thereof, reverted to a state of nature, and have since formed government on the true principles of liberty."

"In fine, this people have suffered every indignity and oppression, that prodigal and lucrative governors, and their swarm of hungry dependants could invent, and carry into execution; and it is surprising, that any persons that live in these days of liberty, still entertain any idea that the said boundary line should operate in favour of the claim of New-York."

"Thus it appears from the great and most universally received maxim in all free governments, that the citizens of Vermont are and ought to be independent of the three governments which lay claim to them; and that every of their said pretensions are daring usurpations and insults on the liberty of an independent, brave and free people, who have never received any governmental protection or benefit from either of them; but instead thereof, have every thing to apprehend from their venality and usurpation."

"Still the people of Vermont, legally speaking, remained under the British government (over which Governor Philip Skeene was commissioned chief magistrate, and next to this government, has the best claim to the jurisdiction of Vermont,) from the 4th day of July 1776, to the 15th day of January next following, and then in a solemn manner disavowed the British government, and rejected the pretensions of Mr. Skeene, and all other pretenders to the jurisdiction of this territory, and declared themselves a free and independent state; and have, as they humbly conceive, in their various struggles for liberty, fairly merited the enjoyment of it: This they consider as the ultimate reward of their many expences, labours, toils, battles, victories and hazards, and for the attainment of which they have chearfully suffered such an uncommon series of concommitant evils."

"And whereas this State hold their charter of liberty from heaven, and not 'of man, or of the will of man' have upon a full and candid examination and consideration determined not to submit heaven-born freedom to the arbitrament of any tribunal below the stars, which through infirmity might deprive them of it: But, as they have closely embraced it in the most critical and hazardous times, are determined to hold it fast, except it be torn from them by the hand of power; which resolution we trust will be justified by the court of heaven and commended by all true friends to the liberty and happiness of mankind."

§

Ethan Allen, Sunderland, to Samuel Huntington, March 9, 1781

"I am confident that Congress will not Dispute my Sincear Attachment to the cause of my Country tho I do not hesitate to say I am fully Grounded in Opinion that Vermont has an Indubitable Right to agree on terms of a Cessation of Hostilities with Great Briton Provided the United States Persist in Rejecting her Application for a Union with them."

"I am as Resolutely Determined to Defend the Independence of Vermont as Congress are that of the United States and Rather than fail will Retire with hardy Green Mountain Boys into the Desolate Caverns of the mountains and wage war with human Nature at large."

§

Ethan Allen, Sunderland, to George Clinton, April 14, 1781

"Col. Ebenezer Allen … and my self are put out of Military Command in the State of Vermont. We are Conceited as to Imagine that Vermont have not Timber to supply our places."

§

The Present State of the Controversy Between the State of New-York and New-Hampshire, on the One Part, and the State of Vermont on the Other (1782)

"It has ever been the practice of the people of Vermont from their first settlement of this disputed territory, to appeal to the impartial judgment of the public as to the justice of their cause, against the claims and demands of contiguous governments to the jurisdiction and right of soil of this territory, and their natural and inherent right to form into a political society, and emancipate into a regular constituted government, as well as to rid themselves from the inconveniences and evils inseparable from a state of nature and anarchy which they had long laboured under, as, to exempt themselves from the usurpation and iron rod of the government of New-York."

"Was it honest in Vermont to extend their jurisdiction upon the states of New-York and New-Hampshire? Previous to the solution of this question, it is requisite to determine whether honesty is trumps or not. Sharp is the word."

"But, say the enemies to the Independence of Vermont, why was there but little or no fighting between them and the enemy in Canada last campaign? Surely there is some negotiation taking place between them inimical to the United States of America—Rouse the whole confederacy and destroy Vermont.—But why, what evil have they sustained from the northward? Have the enemy been permitted to pass through Vermont to invade the United States? No, not yet; but it is going to be done—So is the last trumpet going to sound, but not yet, and it is more than probable that neither of these events will take place in our days."

"There are rumours circulated that the whole confederacy of the United States will join and extirpate Vermont, which is as unlikely as that the tail of the next comet will set the world on fire."

"Vermont does not mean to be so over righteous as by that means to die before her time; but for the State of New-York and New-Hampshire, to stand grip[p]ing their respective claims fast hold of Vermont, and at the same time make such a hedious outcry against the gripe [grip] of Vermont upon them, is altogether romantic and laughable."

❧

Ethan Allen, Sunderland, to Frederick Haldimand, June 16, 1782

"The last refusal of Congress to admit this State Into Union has done more to awaken the common people to a Sense of their Interest and resentment of their Conduct than all which they had done before. By their own act they declare that Vermont does not and shall not belong to the Confederacy. The Consequence is that they may fight their own Battles."

"I shall do everything in my Power to render this State a British province."

❧

Ethan Allen, Guilford, threatening recalcitrant Yorkers, September 10, 1782

"I Ethan Allen do declare that I will give no quarter to the man, woman or child who shall oppose me, and unless the inhabitants of Guilford peacefully submit to the authority of Vermont I swear that I will lay it as desolate as Sodom and Gomorrah by God."

"You have called on your God Clinton till you are tired. Call now on your God Congress and they will answer you as Clinton has done."

ETHAN ALLEN HOMESTEAD, MODERN PHOTO

§

Ethan Allen, Manchester, to Justus Sherwood & Luke Knowlton, April 18, 1783

"I assure you that Vermont are determined not to Unite or Confederate with Congress."

"The Scene is changed and Vermont must do as well as she can and in the menetime feel the highest Obligations to their Friends and will not Confederate with Congress come on what will but will be Independent of Independency."

§

Ethan Allen, Bennington, to Ira Allen, August 31, 1784

"My positive determination is to move to my farm at Onion River as soon as possible and therefore send you the exact dimensions of the House I purpose early in the spring to build that you may without fail git the Bords Sawed according that they may be Seasoned as much as possible. I have plan'd the House 34 x 24 two story High which plan I will not depart from. Early in the Spring I determined to be personally on the premises with the Workmen and provision suitable to Compleat the little Building with all Expedition. ... Do not think that I will change my scheme for the Decree is gone fourth. Therefore let the Boards and provisions be in readiness. From the Philosopher."

§

Ethan Allen, Bennington, "To the Public," November 30, 1784

"I would by no means debar the populus of talking and plotting in politics for this would deprive them of a great share of their happiness and importance."

§

Reason the Only Oracle of Man (1784)

"In the circle of my acquaintance (which has not been small) I have generally been denominated a Deist, the reality of which I have never disputed, being conscious I am no Christian, except mere infant baptism makes me one; and as to being a Deist, I know not strictly speaking, whether I am one or not, for I have never read their writings; mine will therefore determine the matter."

"It is nevertheless to be regretted, that the bulk of mankind, even in those nations which are most celebrated for learning and wisdom, are still carried down the torrent of superstition, and entertain very

REASON
THE ONLY
ORACLE OF MAN,
OR A
Compenduous Syſtem
OF
Natural RELIGION.

Alternately ADORNED with Confutations
of a variety of DOCTRINES
incompatible to it;
Deduced from the moſt exalted Ideas which
we are able to form of the

DIVINE and Human
CHARACTERS,
AND FROM THE
Univerſe in General.

By Ethan Allen, *Eſq*;

BENNINGTON:
STATE OF VERMONT;
Printed by HASWELL & RUSSELL.
M,DCC,LXXXIV.

unworthy apprehension of the being, perfections, creation and providence of GOD, and their duty to him."

"As far as we understand nature, we are become acquainted with the character of God; for the knowledge of nature is the revelation of God. If we form in our imagination a compe[n]duous idea of the harmony of the universe, it is the same as calling God by the name of harmony, for there could be no harmony without regulation, and no regulation without a regulator, which is expressive of the idea of a God."

"Thus it is from the works of nature that we explore its great author; but all inquisitive minds are lost in their searches and researches into the immensity of the divine fullness, from whence our beings and all our blessings flow."

"A belief in those who adhere to that doctrine, that they themselves constitute that blessed number, has been a greater inducement to them to close with it, than all other motives added together. It is a selfish and inferior notion of a God void of justice, goodness and truth, and has a natural tendency to impede the cause of true religion and morality in the world, and diametrically repugnant to the truth of the divine character, and which, if admitted to be true, overturns all religion, wholly precluding the agency of mankind in either their salvation or damnation."

"This doctrine of eternal creation and providence, as also the infinitude of it, may give offence to such persons who may read this book, and who have habituated themselves to trace their genealogy from Adam as the first rational being."

"For as certain as there is a God, he is eternally and infinitely perfect, and if so, his creation and providence is also eternally and infinitely perfect and compleat, whatever our ignorant apprehensions and reasonings on this divine subject may be."

"It may be objected, that immensity, all around the terraqueous ball to the verge of Mose's 'heaven and earth,' had been eternally replete with creation, providence and goodness, but that the part of space comprized in his representation of the 'heavens and earth' was, till the era of its beginning (which according to the chronology of the Jews, was, till less than six thousand years ago) an empty chasm in the creation, and consequently in the providence of God, who so far would be subversive of a just conception of his infinity."

"It has been a great dispute in the schools, whether an ass would not starve to death between two mows, or parcels of choice hay, equally good, and equidistant from him, and but just out of his reach, merely for want of a preponderating motive to chuse to which of the two to apply himself, to satisfy his hunger. However, it is more than probable that the sagacity of the ass in such circumstances, would exceed the theory of those, who in such a case, devote him to death in their speculations."

"When I was a boy, by one means or other, I had conceived a very bad opinion of Pharoah, he seem'd to me to be a cruel despotic Prince, he would give the Israelites straw, but nevertheless demanded of them the full tale of brick; for a time he opposed God Almighty, but was at last luckily drowned in the red sea, at which event, with other good christians, I rejoiced, and even exulted at the overthrow of the base and wicked Tyrant: but after a few years of maturity, and examination of the history of that monarch, given by Moses, with the before recited remarks of the Apostle, I conceived a more favorable opinion of him, in asmuch as we are told that God raised him up, and hardened his heart, and predestinated his reign, his wickedness and overthrow."

"For morality does not derive its nature from books, but from the fitness of things; and though it may be more or less, interspersed through the pages of the Alkoran, its purity and rectitude would remain the same, for that it is founded on eternal right; and whatever writings, books or oral speculations, best illustrate or teach this moral science, should have the preference."

"The superstitious thus set up a spiritual discerning, independent of, and in opposition to reason, and their mere imaginations pass with each other, and with themselves, for infallible truth."

"The period of life is very uncertain, and at the longest is but short: a few years bring us from infancy to manhood, a few more to a dissolution; pain, sickness and death are the necessary consequences of animal life. Through life we struggle with physical evils, which eventually are certain to destroy our earthly composition."

"Reason therefore must be the standard, by which we determine the respective claims of revelation; for otherwise we may as well subscribe to the divinity of the one as of the other, or to the whole of them, or to none at all. So likewise on this thesis, if reason rejects the whole of those revelations, we ought to return to the religion of nature and reason."

"Preposterously absurd would it be, to negative the exercise of reason in religious concerns, and yet, be actuated by it in all other and less occurrences of life."

❦

Ethan's inscription in Fanny Allen's copy of Reason the Only Oracle of Man (1785)

"Dear Fanny wise, the beautiful and young,
The partner of my joys, my dearest self,
My love, pride of my life, your sexes pride,
And pat[tern] of sincere politeness,
To these a welcome compliment I make;
Of treasures rich, the Oracles of Reason."

❦

Ethan Allen, Bennington, to Stephen R. Bradley, September 7, 1785

"I Fancy Sir, you will be diverted when you read the 12th Chapter, it rips up, and overturns the whole notion of Jockeying, alienating, transferring, or imputing of Sin, or Righteousness, from one person to another, and leaves all mankind accountable, for their own moral agency. This is fatal to the Ministerial Damnation Salvation, and their merchandize thereof."

"In order to carry on this Priestcraft, the Clergy must invalidate the law of Nature, Reason is represented as Carnal, and depraved, and the natural State, a condition of mankind, to be damnable, to make way for their mysteries, insperations, and pious frauds, and thus most of the Human race, have been miserably Priest-ridden."

§

Ethan Allen, Bennington, to Zebulon Butler & John Franklin, October 27, 1785

"Avaricious men, make interest their God, and plot against the lives of thousands, to accomplish their mercenary designs."

"Probably the Justice of our claim, will have but little or no effect, on our haughty antagonists, who seek our lands & labours, it may nevertheless inspire us, to defend our rights, with great zeal & fortitude, and serve to make us friends abroade, particularly in Congress, and justifie our opposition, even to blood."

"I hope to see you, face to face, next spring, nor will I give up my interest, to usurpers, without trying it out by force of arms; if we have not fortitude enough to face danger, in a good cause; we are cowards indeed, and must in consequence of it, be slaves, and our posterity, to Pennemitish land thieves., Liberty & Property or slavery and poverty; are now therefore before us, and our Wisdom and fortitude, or Timidity and folly, must terminate the matter."

§

Ethan Allen, Bennington, to Benjamin Stiles, November 16, 1785

"As to my Philosophy … In one of them you read my very soul, for I have not concealed my opinion, nor disguised my sentiments in the least, and however you may, as a severe critic, censer my performance, I presume you will not impeach me with cowardise."

"I expect, that the clergy, and their devotees, will proclaim war with me, in the name of the Lord, his battles they effect to fight, having put on the armour of Faith, the sword of the Spirit and the Artillery of Hell fire. But I am a hardy Mountaineer, and have been accustomed to the dangers and horrors of War, and captivity, and scorn to be intimidated by threats, if they fight me, they must absolutely produce some of their tremendous fire, and give me a sensitive scorching."

§

Ethan Allen, Bennington, to Hector St. John de Crevecoeur, March 2, 1786

"I am not so vain as to imagine that my theology, will afford any considerable entertainment, to the enlightened mind of Mr. St. John, or to any learned Gentlemen in France. Yet it is possible, that he or they, may be Somewhat diverted, with the untutored logic, and Sallies of a mind nursed principally, in the Mountanious wilds of America. And since it is the almost universal foible of mankind, to aspire to something, or other, beyond their natural, or acquired abilities, and as I feel the infection I desire, that Mr. St. John, would lay the oracles of Reason, before the royal academy, & arts and Sciences, at Paris."

"I am however sensible that my reputation, as a reasoner (even in America), will depend in great measure, on the reception that the work may meet with, in the learned Cities, of Paris, and London."

§

Ethan Allen, Wyoming Valley, Pennsylvania, to Matthew Griswold, April 30, 1786

"Law, Order, and Government, are the Hobby Horses of the Pennsylvanians, with which they alias their land schemers, design to dispossess the Connecticut Settlers, and obtain and accumulate to themselves, their lands and labours."

§

Ethan Allen, Sunderland, to Ira Allen, August 18, 1786

"I have not a Copper of money to save me from the Devil. We are rich poor Curst rascals by God. Alter our measures or we shall be a hiss, a proverb, and a bye word, and derision upon Earth."

§

An Address from the Inhabitants of Wyoming . . . to the People at Large of the Commonwealth of Pennsylvania (1786)

"In these scenes of horror, and complicated woe, we were your frontier. Our blood answered for yours. Our hazard and unparalleled distress purchased your safety. We stood between you and the tomahawk and scalping-knife, and diverted the inhuman strokes from you. But, alas! what returns have we had from your government? The widows and orphans, of those who fell in the common cause of America, particularly in your defence, have been plundered, despoiled of their goods, and driven from their habitations, and legal possessions, with other inhabitants in general, and the whole treated nearly as inhumanly, as by the common enemy, and many of our inhabitants have been killed, by the hostile attempts of government, to dispossess us of our lands and labours, without the formality of a tryal by law."

"Your government, hitherto, have been extremely earnest to cram their laws down our throats, and do not fail to hold up to our view, the sanctity thereof, 'The law,' they say, 'is holy, just and good,' but the said inhabitants, *alias* yankees, are carnal, riotous, rebellious, 'and sold under sin,' and their lands and labours must pay for it. In fine the inhabitants of Wyoming, and its vicinity, are so sinful and rebellious, that you gentlemen of the militia of Pennsylvania, must leave your farms and occupations, wives and children, and, at the hazard of your lives, kill and destroy those ugly yankees, who guarded your frontier in the late war, and who, if you do not extirpate, will guard you in a subsequent one."

"That the people of the state at large, have a right to judge, and even interpose in this interesting dispute, will further appear, when by a government (swayed by interested and over-bearing men) they are ordered to march under arms to the hostile ground of Wyoming, and, at the hazard of their lives, fight against us, for no other cause (not reason) but that we will not tamely surrender our farms, orchards, tenements, labours and right of soil, to a junto of land-thieves."

"Their weapons are intrigue and legal deception. Such pious legalists had rather stand aloof in the day of battle, with law books in their hands, and look on and see you, Gentlemen of the Commonality, and those rebellious Yankees, smoke it out at the muzzle of a firelock; and, provided the event of war proves favourable to their claim, to take possession of the land and labours which they have coveted."

"The original design and ultimate end of law is to secure the lives, liberty and property of the subjects. But when government and law are

Burlington 3d of June 1787

Sir

I Embrace this opportunity to write you on the
Subject of wheat or flower a subject of the utmost
moment to Col. Ira and my self it is a pinch with us
and will be so till Harvest pray help us. Ira is
gone to Quaker Danbe and as far as Sunderland
where he has quantities of Pork to bring forward
but we rely on you for the articles of bread till
Harvest as it is not be purchaised in these parts
even for money which by the by is not plenty
with us. My farming business goes on very
brisk but I tremble for bread-corn do not fail
us. I hear my family is well. My compliments
to Mrs Allen. Your Humble Servt

Ethan Allen

Mr Levi Allen

N.B. You can send weat or flower by Mr
McLean's boat by which passage this letter
is conveyed

degenerated in the administration, and subverted to answer the over-bearing, unjust and monopolizing purposes of cruel men, or to dispossess and ruin a large settlement of industrious yeomanry (the supporters of the world of mankind) in such cases the oppressed have a just and natural right to make a bold and manly resistance, agreeably to the greatest of all laws, to wit, that of self-preservation."

❧

Ethan Allen, "Vermont," to Guy Carleton, January 12, 1787

"My Lord, when I speculate on the local situation of this republic to the province of Quebec, its only Seaport, and that the lumber, and other articles of export, as well as those of import of this little commonwealth, must be navigated by the river St. Laurence, it appears to me, that nature has situated the Inhabitants of these territories, to be friends and neighbors."

"I am apprehensive that I am unhappy in my genius, having rose above the vulgar superstition of the human race, and yet fallen, below the understanding of the learned and wise."

❧

Ethan Allen, Bennington, to Hector St. John de Crevecoeur, April 14, 1787

"Our Country is situated in a Good Holesome Climate, our Soil Produces richly of every kind of the Groth of North America, our Settlement by Emigration from the other States & from Urope is very Rapid, the Wealth of the State increases fast, & in fine our present

Government is the best & most Regular & freest from Debt of any part of America."

❦

Ethan Allen, Burlington, to Stephen R. Bradley, November 9, 1787

"A dead man often times has such accounts brought in against his Estate which Bashfulness would have prevented had he been alive."

❦

Ethan Allen, Burlington, to Stephen R. Bradley, November 16, 1787

"I have lately arrived at my new farm of 14 hundred acres in one body which are three hundred & fifty acres of choice River Intervale a quanty of swaley and rich upland meadow interspersed with the finest of wheat land and pasture land well watered and is by nature equal to any tract of land of the same number of acres that I ever saw."

"Little is said about Philosophy here our 'talk is of Bullocks and our glory is in the gad,' we mind Earthly things."

❦

Ethan Allen, Burlington, to Levi Allen, November 28, 1787

"Mrs. Allen was brought to bed on the 24th instant with hearty well looking Boy, she is as well as could be expected. I wish you would send me a cag of old spirits and Some loaf and brown Sugar on this occasion."

§

Ethan Allen, Quebec, to Guy Carleton, July 16, 1788

"Your Lordship is undoubtedly sensible of the Jealousy of the United States over Vermont, since it is not and will not be confederated with them. They proceed so far as to threaten its subjugation, as soon as they have established their new proposed constitution and made their government sufficiently energetic."

"Vermont could on emmergency bring fifteen thousand able effective men into the field, who in point of prowes, would probably more than equal a like number of the troops of the United States, especially defending themselves against the usurpation of those states."

"In the time of General Haldimand's command, could Great Britain have afforded Vermont protection, they would readily have yielded up their independency, and have become a province of Great Britain. And should the United States attempt a conquest of them, they would, I imagine, do the same, should the British policy harmonize with it. For the leading men in Vermont are not sentimentally attached to a republican form of government, till they can have a better, and hope that they will be able to do it, as long as the united States will be able to maintain theirs, or till they can on principles of mutual Interest and advantage, return to the British government without war or annoyance from the United States."

§

Ethan Allen, Burlington, to John Wheelock, August 25, 1788

"Sir since our interview at Bennington, I have almost catched an Idea of a mear spirit, or unbodied Soul, but not quite."

"A compatency of knowledge in the sciences, is therefore our only Bulwork, against Superstition and Idolatry. The Superstitious part of mankind, which by one means or other, are far the most numerous, are but the dupes of Church and State, at their command they cut one anothers throats, as they suppose for Gods sake, and commit all manner of cruel[t]y and outrage."

Ethan Allen

How his contemporaries saw him

❧

Charles Hutcheson, Yorker of Rupert, October 1771

"Deponent is also credibly Inform'd that said Allen Denys the Being of a God & Denys that there is any Infernal Spirit existing."

❧

Lieut. Jocelyn Feltham, Fort Ticonderoga, May 1775

"This person Ethan Allen and [Seth] Warner are as great villains as any on earth."

❧

Philip Schuyler to Congress, October 5, 1775

"I am very apprehensive of disagreeable consequences arising from Mr. Allen's imprudence. I always dreaded his impatience of subordination."

❧

Capt. Alexander Graydon on Ethan Allen as British prisoner in New York City, 1776-77

"His figure was that of a robust, large-framed man, worn down by confinement and hard fare; but he was now recovering his flesh and spirits; and a suit of blue clothes, with a gold laced hat that had been presented to him by the gentlemen of Cork, enabled him to make a very passable appearance for a rebel colonel. … I have seldom met with a man, possessing, in my opinion, a stronger mind, or whose mode of expression was more vehement and oratorical. Notwithstanding that Allen might have something of the insubordinate, lawless frontier spirit in his composition … he appeared to me to be a man of generosity and honor."

❧

George Washington, May 1778

"His fortitude and firmness seem to have placed him out of reach of misfortune. There is an original something in him that commands admiration; and his long captivity and sufferings have only served to increase if possible, his enthusiastic zeal."

❧

Lord George Germaine to Sir Henry Clinton, December 1778

"[Ethan Allen is] a person of infamous character and wicked practices. … But under the present circumstances it may be that he can be attracted."

❧

Levi Allen in the Connecticut Courant, March 2, 1779

"The truth is, I have been unfortunate as to have a dispute with Ethan Allen, (my brother) but as it respected property only hoped it had subsided on account of the many well known services rendered him while a prisoner in the hands of a cruel enemy; and am most sensibly affected on finding it has had no other effect on him, only to make his attacks more severe, and of a more public nature."

❧

Samuel Minott, eastside Yorker, Spring 1779

"Our situation is truly critical and distressing, we therefore beseach your Excellency to take the most speedy and effectual measures for our Relief; otherwise our Person and Property must be at the disposal of Ethan Allen which is more to be dreaded than Death with all its Terrors."

❧

Jeremy Belknap, New Hampshire historian, 1779

"I think him an original in his way… as rough and boisterous as the scenes he has passed through."

❧

John Williams to Gov. George Clinton, July 1780

"As for Allen he swears that he will fight, nay even run on to the mountains and live on mouse meat before he will subject himself to New York or Congress."

§

Frederick Haldimand, Quebec, to Sir Henry Clinton, August 13, 1780

"I have taken much Pains, by Prisoners and intelligent Loyalists, to discover if anything might be effected with Allen, and the people of Vermont—I am assured by all, that no dependence can be had in him—his character is well known, and his followers, or dependents, are a collection of the most abandoned wretches that ever lived, to be bound by no Laws or Ties."

§

James Rogers, St. John, Canada, to R. Mathews, September 1780

"I am informed that Mr. Allen of the State of Vermont has declaired if the Congress will not allow him to have an independent State he will join them that will."

§

Sir Henry Clinton to Duke of Gloucester, December 14, 1780

"It appears that Ethan Allen has joined the King's troops. I have been for these two years tempting that chief, and I have offered him what Congress have refused him."

§

Justus Sherwood, Isle aux Noix, to Frederick Haldimand, February 1781

"The above report puts me in suspense between fear and hope for Allen is sincere and matters are drawing to a favorable conclusion much faster than I ever expected. Or he is a most subtle designing fellow. I am not able to determine which."

❧

Ann Bleecker, Albany, New York, December 1781

"General Allen was bound up in gold-lace and felt himself grand as the Great Mogul."

❧

Peter Allen, Loyalist, 1781

"Ethan Allen was of Connecticut also; of a bad Character, & had been guilty of Actions bad enough to forfeit even a good one. He was brave, but unprincipled; & after he had been a prisoner in Canada, sent to England in Irons, as a Rebel, & afterwards dismissed, he openly acknowledged, when he was at *Falmouth,* that it was indifferent to him for whom he fought; whether the King of *Great Britain,* the King of *Spain* or for *America;* they who would give him the best Pay should have his Service. . . . This Man seems to be so overstocked with Honor, that there will never be an End of its Dissipation."

❧

T. Baker & D. Lamb, Eastside Yorkers, September 1782

"[Ethan Allen] said that he could go to Albany and be head monarch if he had but orders in three weeks, and he had a good mind to do it, and further Allyn God damned Clinton over and over from time to time."

❧

Bennington Vermont Gazette advertisement, September 19, 1785

"Just imported in the Balloon Sarcastic (Imported from France) and now opening for sale … by the Genius of Vermont at her store on the top of Mount Anthony in Bennington, a large assortment of valuable books, among which are the following … Deism Confessed and Good Manners Defended, with a chapter in favor of Oracles and a section on the heat of good blood near the grand clymacterice, and the animation of youthful charms."

❧

Ethan Allen gravestone, Burlington, 1789

"The Corporeal Part of Ethan Allen Rests Beneath
this Stone, the 12th day of Feb. 1789, Aged 50
Years. His spirit tried the
Mercies of his God
In Whom he firmly Trusted."

❧

Rev. Ezra Stiles diary entry, February 28, 1789

"Died in Vermont the profane and impious Deist Ethan Allen. And in Hell he lifts up his eyes, being in Torments."

§

Rev. Nathan Perkins journal entry, May 26, 1789

"Arrived at Onion-river falls & passed by Ethan Allyn's grave. An awful Infidel, one of the wickedest men that ever walked this guilty globe. I stopped & looked at his grave with a pious horror."

§

Rev. Uzal Ogden, 1789

"Allen was a profane and ignorant Deist, who died with a mind replete with horror and despair."

§

Lemuel Hopkins, "On General Ethan Allen," 1793

"Lo Allen 'scaped from British jails,
His tushes broke by biting nails.
Appears in hyperborean skies,
To tell the world the bible lies."

"Behold him move, ye staunch divines!
His tall head bustling through the pines;
All front he seems like wall of brass,
And brays tremendous as an ass;
One hand is clench'd to batter noses,
While t'other scrawls 'gainst Paul and Moses."

§

John A. Graham, A Descriptive Sketch of the Present State of Vermont (1796)

"General Allen believed, or affected to believe, with Pythagoras, that man after death would transmigrate into beasts, fish, fowls, and reptiles, and I have often heard him affirm, that he should live again under the form of a large white horse, which I suppose was his favourite colour in that animal. Yet not withstanding these his wild ideas of Religion and futurity, it is barely justice to declare, that in all his moral dealings and concerns, Ethan Allen possessed the strictest sense of honour, integrity, and uprightness."

§

John J. Henry, An Accurate and Interesting Account of the Hardships and Sufferings of That Band of Heroes Who Traversed the Wilderness in the Campaign Against Quebec in 1775 (1812)

"[Ethan Allen] was a man of much peculiarity of character. Large, powerful of body, a most ferocious temper, (feared neither God nor man,) of a most daring courage, and pertinacity of disposition, which was unconquerable, and very astonishing in all his undertakings: withal he had the art of making himself beloved, and revered by all his followers."

§

Timothy Dwight, Travels in New-York and New-England (1821)

"[Ethan Allen's] education was confined, and furnished him with a mere smattering of knowledge, but his mind was naturally haughty, restless, and enterprising. Licentious in his disposition, he was impatient of the restraints either of government or religion, and not always submissive to those of common decency. In his conversation he was voluble, blunt, coarse and profane; in his pretensions to knowledge, daring; and in his assertions, bold and peremptory. The confidence which he seemed to possess in himself naturally inspired confidence in others still less informed, and they readily believed that he who asserted so positively must be sure that his assertions were true."

"When it [*Reason the Only Oracle of Man*] came out, I read as much of it as I could summon patience to read. Decent nonsense may possibly amuse an idle hour, but brutal nonsense can only be read as an infliction of penal justice. The style was crude and vulgar, and the sentiments were coarser than the style. The arguments were flimsy and unmeaning, and the conclusions were fastened upon the premises by mere force."

Bibliography

Ethan Allen and eighteenth-century Vermont have attracted the attention of many writers. This short list is a selection from the available titles; for the full range of published books, pamphlets and articles on the Allens and early Vermont history, readers should consult T. D. S. Bassett, *Vermont: A Bibliography of Its History* (Boston: G. K. Hall & Co., 1981) and its several updates in the Committee for a New England Bibliography's state and regional series.

An asterisk preceding a listing denotes a principal source of quotations in this collection.

§

*Allen, Ethan. *Reason the Only Oracle of Man* (1784; reprint ed., New York: Burt Franklin, 1972).

Bellesiles, Michael A. *Revolutionary Outlaws: Ethan Allen and the Struggle for Independence on the Early American Frontier* (Charlottesville: University Press of Virginia, 1993).

*Duffy, John J. et al., eds. *Ethan Allen and His Kin: Correspondence, 1772–1819* (Hanover: University Press of New England, 1998), 2 volumes.

Fox, Dixon Ryan. *Yankees and Yorkers* (New York: New York University Press, 1940).

*Graffagnino, J. Kevin, ed. *Ethan and Ira Allen: Collected Works* (Benson, Vt.: Chalidze Publications, 1992), 3 volumes.

Jellison, Charles A. *Ethan Allen: Frontier Rebel* (Syracuse, N.Y.: Syracuse University Press, 1969).

JONES, MATT B. *Vermont in the Making, 1750-1777* (1939; reprint ed., Camden, Ct.: Archon Books, 1968).

PELL, JOHN. *Ethan Allen* (Boston: Houghton Mifflin, 1929).

SHALHOPE, ROBERT E. *Bennington and the Green Mountain Boys: The Emergence of Liberal Democracy in Vermont, 1760-1850* (Baltimore: The Johns Hopkins University Press, 1996).

SHERMAN, MICHAEL, ed. *A More Perfect Union: Vermont Becomes a State, 1777-1816* (Montpelier: Vermont Historical Society & Vermont Statehood Bicentennial Commission, 1991).

WILLIAMSON, CHILTON A. *Vermont in Quandary: 1763-1825* (Montpelier: Vermont Historical Society, 1949).

About the Vermont Historical Society

The Vermont Historical Society is the only institution in Vermont that collects artifacts and documents that reflect the entire history of the state, every geographical area, and every chronological period, including the present.

The museum collections consist of more than 20,000 artifacts of Vermont history from precontact times to the present. Some 50,000 catalogued books and serial titles, 1,800 linear feet of manuscripts, 30,000 photographs, 1,000 maps, 8,700 broadsides, and other printed ephemera as well as film, microfilm, and oral history tapes related to Vermont, regional history, and New England genealogy constitute the library's collections.

Founded in 1838 by an act of the Vermont state legislature, the Society is an independent membership organization, governed by a board of trustees. Today, its mission is to collect, preserve, and interpret those things—works of art, artifacts, books, documents, manuscripts, and photographs—that serve to illustrate the history of Vermont and its place within the larger context of American life. The Society maintains a diverse, wide-ranging educational outreach program designed especially for teachers, primary and secondary students, and the general public. The Society coordinates the state contest of National History Day, a program that encourages students to do primary research. Each summer it sponsors the Vermont History Expo, a two-day event featuring exhibits from more than 100 local historical societies, speakers, performers, artisans, reenactors, games, and more.

❧

www.vermonthistory.org

❧

Vermont Historical Society Museum

MONTPELIER

Experience yesterday *today* at the Vermont Historical Society's new permanent exhibit. Find your story in "Freedom and Unity: One Ideal, Many Stories." All ages will love the full range of Vermont's unique history, with displays ranging from an Abenaki structure and a colonial tavern to an old-time railroad station and a World War Two living room, and much more. Come away with a piece of history from the museum's gift shop, too. Exhibit open 10-4, Tuesday-Saturday (all year), Sundays 12-4 (May-October only), in the Pavilion Building, 109 State St., Montpelier, VT 05609-0901, 802-828-2291. VHS members and children under 6 free; adult nonmembers $5; seniors, students, and children $3. **Field trips and group tours are encouraged.**

❧

Vermont Historical Society Library

BARRE

The Vermont Historical Society collects, preserves, and makes available to the public a wide variety of library materials documenting the history and people of Vermont. Library hours: Tuesday-Friday, 9-4:30, second Saturday of each month, 9-4. Research fee: $5/person per day; VHS members and students, free. Located in the newly renovated Vermont History Center at 60 Washington St., Barre, VT 05641-4209, 802-479-8500.

§

Recent Publications of the Vermont Historical Society

ROBERT L. MCCULLOUGH, *Crossings: A History of Vermont Bridges* (2005)

MICHAEL SHERMAN, GENE SESSIONS, and P. JEFFREY POTASH, *Freedom and Unity: A History of Vermont* (2004)

DEBORAH P. CLIFFORD, *The Passion of Abby Hemenway: Memory, Spirit, and the Making of History* (2001)

T. D. SEYMOUR BASSETT, *The Gods of the Hills: Piety and Society in Nineteenth-Century Vermont* (2000)

J. KEVIN GRAFFAGNINO, SAMUEL B. HAND, and GENE SESSIONS, EDS., *Vermont Voices, 1609 Through the 1990s: A Documentary History of the Green Mountain State* (1999)

GIRO PATALANO, *Behind the Iron Horse: The People Who Made the Trains Run in the Bellows Falls, Vermont, Area (1941-1980)* (1997)

ESTHER MUNROE SWIFT, *Vermont Place-Names: Footprints of History*, 2nd ed. (1996)

DAVID LUDLUM, *The Vermont Weather Book*, rev. ed. (1996)

MICHAEL SHERMAN, ED., *A More Perfect Union: Vermont Becomes a State, 1777-1816* (1991)

About The Ethan Allen Homestead

In February 1784, Ethan Allen, a widower for about a year, married Frances (Fanny) Montresor, a young, vivacious, and attractive woman of 24. Allen's whirlwind courtship and marriage to the spirited young widow may have influenced his request a little over six months later in August to his brother Ira to saw boards for a 24′ x 34′, two-story house. Ethan planned to construct the house in the Burlington intervale on land acquired in a swap with Ira. He would build it set back from the Winooski River and commanding a view of Ira's larger house across the river in Colchester. Around the homestead he planned to establish a "new farm of 14 hundred acres in which are three hundred & fifty acres of choice River Intervale." The tract, Allen wrote, included "swaley and rich upland meadow interspersed with the finest of wheat land and pasture land well watered" that he asserted "is by nature equal to any tract of land of the same number of acres that I ever saw."

Ethan moved Fanny, who would deliver the second of their three children that November, and the three surviving children from his first marriage to their new home in July 1787. By then he had 40 acres under cultivation. "Little is said about Philosophy" on the farm, he wrote, "here our 'talk is of Bullocks and our glory is in the gad [a cattle prod].'" With his young wife and growing family, Allen apparently found contentment with the routine of farm life that he restlessly had rejected as a youth. On February 11, 1789, Allen the farmer set out for his cousin Ebenezer Allen's farm in South Hero with one of his hired men in an ox-drawn hayrack to get fodder for his livestock. Returning home the next day, Ethan "was taken with a fit" and fell into a coma. He never regained consciousness, and he died at the homestead that afternoon.

In 1975, historian, author, and long-time senior editor of *Vermont Life* Ralph Nading Hill announced that he had found Ethan Allen's homestead. Hill worked with a group of "Founders" to secure ownership of the structure and surrounding land adjacent to property of the Winooski Valley Park District. At the same time, he led a team that stripped away nearly two centuries of change and additions to return Ethan Allen's last home to its original dimensions. Subsequent restoration and detailed physical analysis have established the authenticity of the Ethan Allen Homestead.

In 1982 Ralph Hill and a group of associates formed the Ethan Allen Homestead Trust, formalizing the organization in 1985. In 1989 the Trust opened the Homestead to the public and it has since maintained and conserved the property. The Trust uses the Homestead as a vehicle for public and school programs about a broad range of Vermont's early heritage in general and the life and work of Ethan Allen, Vermont's most recognized citizen, in particular.

~